despite GRAVITY

A Collection of Poems

by Phillip Mulligan

PALMETTO
P U B L I S H I N G
Charleston, SC
www.PalmettoPublishing.com

Paperback ISBN: 9798998698613

Other Books by Phillip Mulligan

My Life as a Poem: A Collection of Poems
by Phillip Mulligan, Photographs by Susan Morse

A Year of Mornings: A Collection of Poems
by Phillip Mulligan, Photographs by Susan Morse
Published by Messenger Street Press, Lebanon, NH

Cover Photo by Steve Heap, Backyard Image Photography
Cover Design by Susan Morse

APPRECIATIONS

This collection of poems started years ago in the Chelsea, Vermont library, where our writers' group met for years followed by another in Corinth and now in Lebanon, NH. The listening and encouragement of readers and writers has kept me going. Thank you to all who have listened and read these poems. Extra thanks go to my final readers Clyde Watson, Catherine Tudish and Sarah Caouette and sweeping bows to my invaluable in-house editor and book designer, Susan Morse, who knows me and my poems so well.

CONTENTS

TWO

THREE

FOUR

ONE

Fragile Hope

Granite killdeer eggs
on a shoal of speckled stones

invisible
to all but nature's geologist

who laid her most fragile hope
in a nest as hard as rock.

Waiting for a Sign

Blue grain-less linoleum
pasted to the morning sky
erases any hint of the heavens

grass of the field holds
the position of paint

birds clutch their nests as breezes
lie still under bushes
beside the watching rabbit

until somehow it begins,
a breath of reluctant leaves gesture

the twitching squirrel no longer waits
to consider the walnut

and a small hole in the eastern sky
opens with apologies
to reveal the generosity of our star
ninety million miles away.

A Gift

In daylight my candle burns
I sit to see what comes
and it is a nuthatch.

Into my window it flies
becoming trapped between sashes
caught like a specimen under microscope glass.

I catch it once by the tail
a feather comes free and I let it go.

I catch it once by the wing
it's too fragile and I let it go.

I catch it once by the shoulder
gently pull the tiny bird between the mullions
cradle it in my hands

then open them to the outside,
three feathers left behind
in the window's cobweb.

A message

every touch, every sound, every dream
dam them - they overflow
divert them - they are back at my feet

gifts, I don't know from where
how to unwrap them
or what they are once I do.

It's a nuthatch.
Let it go.

Confluence

Tributaries transect land
to gather the rain, like veins
they pull to the heart
all that lets go.

Tides wait
wondering what takes so long
but is there any rush
when there is so far to go?

Springs, seeps and gurgles gather,
in them lives what gives us life,
the water, like wine
reveals the edge of flow and solid ground.

Playful ripple rills of belief
raucous rapids of passion
deep stillness, all become us
though sometimes they may be bridged
if one chooses not to wade.

Come to the merge and meet
feel the pull
be joined as waters deepen
carry what follows and floats above.

Meet at the fork
come down tine to handle
melt into my arms as I will yours,
together we will see the sea.

My Family Measures Rain

Like disciples in drought and fools in flood
my family collects and measures rain.
We gauge what falls as an offering
not from God, not in that way,
in more of a tangible way, where we are here
and the rain is there, and sometimes
it falls and we feel lucky
to catch some going by.

My father measured rain.
If it fell, the gauge by the pear tree would steal
seven square inches worth from the sky
and funnel the captive waters into a cylinder calibrated
with tick marks along its side.
Like a chemist, he would lift the cylinder level with his eyes
read the meniscus and then with a sweep of his arm
free the water to the ground.
In the office, a spiral notebook, the smallest they made
received date and data.

It doesn't help a farmer to measure rain.
It falls. It doesn't.
No association, ration or allocation
just heaven's offering, if we believed in heaven.
Instead we believe in nimbus clouds and rain shadows
swirls of high pressure, low pressure
and sap rising.

My family talks in inches, tenths and hundredths.
After a storm it isn't, how are you when we greet
we ask how much did you get.
Envy, pride or sometimes disbelief is followed
with an assessment of crops, seedbeds and streams.
My family measures rain in reservoirs
of corn and hay, oak and hickory
squash and cabbage, wheat and rich dung;
in this way
we believe in rain.

Waterborne

Three stones cut by frost and coaxed by currents
still hold their mother's image,
tops broader than my arms spread wide
muddy bottoms farther than I could reach
down the shear sliced stone.

In the cleaved canyon cuts
I captained boats of bark
where the current ran calm.
My mother, silent beside me
listened without reply.
Sometimes I joined her,
the boats breaking for
rolling waters.

Always Joking

Twelve oranges giggle in a wooden bowl
they are up to something,
I know they are too nice to tease me
but they are not beyond a practical joke.

I look to my left and then to my right
for any funny business,
nothing seems out of place
then I smile
they got me
I am being suspicious of citrus.

Commencement

Before it has finished its work
robins break the night-spell
with impatience and impunity,
I try to ignore them
but the song sparrow agrees
as does the phoebe and finch
and I know that this sleep is over.

They are right of course
summer is no time to sleep
as it pours out over the fields of ripening hay,
now is the time when all have work to do
make its nut
fledge its young
capture the long light and pack it away into bales
for a time that seems unimaginable
except for the fact that it happens every year.

Reluctantly I rise
testing yesterday's muscles
Never Mind Them! the robin sings
Come Out! the phoebe insists
and I do

into the morning's mist
that drifts half lit and listless
as the sun is yet to break
which it will do in its own time
regardless of the avian enthusiasm.

Morning Responsibilities

Responsibilities are ever-present.
They get out of bed before I do. They dress for success
brush their teeth and comb their hair, they smile into
the mirror self-aware and self-assured, without breakfast
they are ready to go. Because of all their racket
I pull myself upright and dress in yesterday's clothes.
I go to the sink and brush my teeth
think my hair looks ok and head downstairs.
The Responsibilities have the coffee on, I wanted tea.
They have the radio tuned to the news, I wanted Bach

Responsibilities are so earnest.
With admirable and annoying determination, Phone-Calls
stands in front of Check-the-Weather and Feed-the-Chickens
holding a paper covered with names and numbers I must call
before I leave. Emails holds my laptop in their out-stretched
hand and rolls their eyes at Phone-Calls while being pushed
to the side by Walk-the-Dog. Do-the-Laundry, whom no one
likes, is standing stock still in the middle of everything with
the overflowing hamper, their strategy of gathering attention
includes always being in the way. Lunch is near the back of
the crowd waving a loaf of bread over their head. They are
right I will need a sandwich today.

Never a self-starter, Build-a-Fire is shivering on top
of the wood stove with a match in their hand.

Responsibilities groan and grin, moan and mince.
The phone rings and Phone-Calls raises their arms in jubilant
victory when I move to answer it. Bickering ensues.
I quiet everyone to furtive grumbling by placing my hand
over the receiver and giving them a no-bull-shit stare before
lifting it to my ear. My side of the conversation is overheard.
Monday the 15th, yes, I think I can make that, I say.
Calendar immediately pushes through the crowd with
a self-satisfied smile carrying my day planner. They put
it down on the table open to the correct month and point
to the day in question. Yes, I am free. I will see you then, I say
barely keeping my irritation at Calendar from my voice.

Responsibilities have a high sense of self-regard.
When I hang up, the clamor resumes. Snow-Shoveler
holds their bright orange scoop over their head calling out
Twelve inches in the driveway! Breakfast wants a bite
of the action and is juggling 2 eggs with moderate success.
Feed-the-Cat must be sleeping in because Filene has her claws
dug into the Carhartt canvas of my pants and isn't letting go.
These ridiculous demons proclaim their loyalty and say
they are here to help, but I have had enough. I fool
Clean-the-House into giving me their broom and use it

to sweep them all, including the cat, out to the woodshed
where they can stack wood, while I stay inside
change the radio station and pour a cup of tea.

Farmer Jive

Vivid in my memory is Mike driving down the farm lane
a track in the field of ruts and protruding cobbles.
He is on the Farmall 300 with the lugged tires
rolling up the road from either side of him,
without fenders they are close, but he is fine
he rides with a horseman's seat
and grips the steering wheel.

The tractor softens some of the bumps
with its rubber tires but others make it through,
from my view by the shop, the seat
which sits atop an eight-inch tapered coil spring
bounces with playful kindness.

Mike rides with supple spine and hips
rocking right, rolling left
while his head bobs in un-choreographed syncopation.
He is unaware that I am watching
but it makes no difference
it's just how he rides.

Spring Migration

Free of ice, the path is clear
and now the banks are brim full.
Down the fall line
pulled by gravity
by passion and mission
awakened water moves
with the deliberation of spring.

Though most snow has melted
molecules of water emerge
from under the rocks
up through the mud
down from the sky,
like a murmuration of birds
they move in unison
into brooks and streams
grow into rivers
careen over escarpments
over dams and through raceways,
if there are enough of them
they will ignore the oxbows
and flood the flats.
Rocks, stumps, even trees

that are in the path
are met with fury
uprooted and then swept along
day and night in the endless stream.

Down, down, down
numbers at each tributary
swell in a lumbering crescendo
until they arrive at a place
vast and familiar, singular and whole
sweet with salt and hugged by the moon
a homecoming, a communion
with all who have joined
the order of the Ocean.

Despite Gravity

Poplar fluffs float by me
on a breeze only they can see.
Could their lightness be so slight
they never touch the ground?

They show no concern for this
or the weight of the code they carry
which holds a whole tree inside.

TWO

Packing Out

We are moving, I say to no one
ignoring my catatonic state.
I'd pause for reflection
but the mirror's been packed
so I think of playing my harmonica
then restrain myself from making
what would only be a sorrowful sound.

Sorting and packing has everything on edge
the books are huddling in boxes
the huddling boxes have our dog nervous
and I am fretting because I don't know if
I am hanging on or letting go.

There's so much sorting
safety pins from paperclips
computer cords from sunglass lanyards
unread magazines from unread books,
the harmonica, that I have never played
has been sorted three times
and still lies on the desk
with no place to go.

I have three choices when sorting
Trash, Giveaway, Save.
Trash is old phones, and pencils under five inches long
and all the three ring binders.
Giveaway is half of my pens, a potted plant
and maybe the harmonica.

Saves are what remain,
old topo maps with notes
annotated choral music
generously decorated birthday cards from our kids.
Maybe when I am ninety I'll tape
all these things to my nursing room wall.

In the filing cabinet
old business cards show up,
remember I was a reiki practitioner, a mediator
a corporate communications trainer? Ha !
Clearly business hung on my hammer
proven by pounds of house plans
energy audits, kitchen designs, bills
and receipts- now Trash.

What's left, besides tax returns my accountant

says I must keep, are personal papers
like the beginnings of a play I couldn't write
or the fading photo of Lyda the cow
and me with our red ribbon.

We are moving, I say to myself out loud.
Get moving.

Bedrocks

An earth-stained foundation stone
cleaned of leaves and soil
holds our house like its mountain.

It stayed as we built around it.
Now buttress and indoor artifact,
rain and cold no longer weather
its immutable crystals.

Like our horse Prince,
pasture rain rolling off his back
the snow sliding,
standing draft solid, still and black.
Holding home.
Only he, if brought inside
wouldn't stay.

In My Absence

While I was away a beach chair sat
staring at the fog-strewn water

surely it saw birds, probably a boat
possibly fish jumping

when I returned, no recollection
no acknowledgement

as if nothing happened
as if it weren't there

maybe it's no matter
maybe the fish didn't jump.

Old Roots

Trees grow freely here
mob grazing old fields until their grass is gone
if not chased back to the wood's edge
by stock or tool.

I know some see this as a loss
the hard work
the clearing, the stumping, the stoning
fourteen-hour days of backbreak
left to leave, no trace
save for a dead furrow, maybe a harrow tooth,
a windrow of stones.

A field of activity
becomes a copse of quiet weaving roots.
Why didn't the farmers feel the loss
and send their cattle?
Why didn't we brush hog more views?

In the end the trees wanted it more
and work to fill a vague memory of before
when springs weren't mud holes
and ephemerals floated safely in canopied shade

when soils soaked in the rain
and toadstools and mosses grew
a time before the web of centuries was felled
and shipped
and burned
and milled.

Fog's Closet

Fog steals time and tucks it away
into its quiet closet of other things
it finds unnecessary
like sun hats and sharp edges,
color and ambition.

Disarmed, these things sit mutely on shelves
only the sun tests the latch
and peeks out through the keyhole
to see if the coast is clear.

foreign land

where my compass declinates
cardinal points obtuse
I stipple over sidewalk cracks

sounds bounce
hit me in the knees, nose and toes
I twist towards them,
they won't fit in my ear

as if I knew where I was in the world
and painted a sunrise in the east
though really everybody's west
and my night their day

Reluctant Eulogy to a Man I Loved

Mark,
whose eyes twinkled and laughed with honest joy
you left us with such fondness and confusion
in the early morning when you couldn't see the sun rise
or you didn't want to
or it simply hurt too much.

Mark,
I am not alone in this hole of sadness but because
you have rearranged the landscape I thought we
had mapped together I feel lonely
and worried that the mud holes I jump over
are calderas of quicksand.

Mark,
I too have a hunting rifle whose clip of ammunition
lies safely separated from its firing pin
and like you, I too know where they both dwell.
I wonder if you thought before then, or even
at the time that a bullet could save you and
leave me behind wounded.

Mark,
I understand grief is solitary and hope
can feel like a luxury in dark times.
I understand the danger of self-harm lies sometimes close
but how could it ever cure the pain?
Maybe your brain tripped and your balance faltered just
at the moment you were supposed to step on the stone
the dry one
in the muddy trail.

Some People are Trees

Long ago I pulled a tap root of generations
and sailed east like a downy seed
to a field in Chelsea Vermont
where I landed and stayed
for what some would call quite-a-while.
Though I settled, built a home, raised a family
I learned from the deep hole I left behind
what planted means
and I am not a tree.

A tree never moves
it may twist and sway to shed storms
or dig deep to overcome drought
but it won't leave
it casts its lot once
holds its ground come what may.

I know people bound to land
cleaved with community
rooted in family
these people are part of the landscape
that I pass through.
I am not a tree

but a seed
a fresh start
a beginning, an end, a beginning again
while others hold the ground.

Ephemeral

We are cautious this morning
for fear of being fooled by Spring.
She has floated in
maybe on a whim she will stay today
find some time to preen
then lightly sleep amongst the hepatica
while we wait for her gaze, a smile
and feel blessed she's come
even for a while,
it will only be for a little while.

They Are Hiding Right in Front of Me

like sparkling stars in a noon blue sky
like drops of water in a rain filled lake
like silence in the din of day
they wait
hoping we will stop to listen
hoping our eyes close to see

Origin of Orange

Just as I am about to eat the orange
I saved for this special moment
I am interrupted by a question of great
and immediate importance.
Was the orange named before or after the color?
I ponder this as I look at its near impossible hue.

Gold, a color and a mineral
silver, bronze and copper too
all good company I think for my fruit
and then, as if I were an animal of the wild
I drive my thumb deep into the fleshy orange skin.

It fights back like a squid
blinding me with citrus oil, but I don't care
all interest in etymology has vanished.
I intuitively perform the craniotomy
revealing the citro-campus, the citro-bellum
and the reptilian Anita Bryant-oblongata.

I rip a section of the citrus into my mouth,
the flavor is so bright
so bursting with brilliance
I am freed of mind and questions.
In my ecstasy, I know
Orange, the fruit, came first.

Bacchanal

When the summer tide is high, heat hits the headwall
pushing the limits of sultry to bushy and tangled.
Soon it will slide back, but before it does
there is one more reverie
one more sonic bloom.

Reminiscent of vernal pools' amphibious trill
fields flood with dry scratching legs
and chitin wings as insects ravish
the intoxicated air
in humid-thick rapture.

A bacchanalia of crickets,
cicadas and katydids
hang from trees, flail through the air
and jam the airwaves
with sex and seduction

until in sweat, swelter and abandon
the season releases itself from its burgeon
of renewal and responsibility
and falls slack
on autumn's receding wave.

THREE

High Water

The rains come way too hard and rivers rise
once above their banks
they run like a dog that broke its chain
right, then left, then through
digging and piling
floating a forest of sticks and trees into town
then dropping them out on the flats, broken.

After the flush residents emerge to gawk

that's Frank's fuel tank in the park
Betsy's garden shed under the bridge
Paul's deck in Vida's backyard
all covered with mud, slick and saturated
smelling of pond bottoms, old oil and rankled duff.
It's everywhere, to be shoveled
hosed and bucketed
thick with all the clouds could loosen.

So Random

Catching it just happened without thinking.
I saw a flash
I put up my hand and *Thwap!*
my fingers closed around a meteorite.

Fresh from far off space
it sat there in my palm,
neither of us had a clue
what to do next.

Turning Point

It was the moment the car couldn't contain me
that I stopped like an emergency
left it by the broken road and
rolled under the barbed wire
into the prairies' sward long with hope.
Welcomed with aria and alleluia I rose
sky and contour pulling me towards their meeting place
of loess and wind; the horizon's laughter
almost touchable in vale, but oh so far
when I broke the rise.
Down in swale, up to apogee
each time I crested I had miles to go.

The surge of inspiration now tempered,
atop a prairie roll I look back.
My grass path is lined with stems
genuflecting like aspirants following me
as if I had been touched by the divine.
Have I been making or following this trail,
I thought I knew.

The expanse ahead tag-teases the hills behind
but they will never catch up.
The grasses that followed me
will disperse wind-washed and disappointed.
Do they know that without them I would be lost?

Incredulous

Belief, loud line in the sand
don't leap with faith in the heat of the day
and leave me flat-footed to take your punches.
Drop the fighting words,
ask me what I know,
and you will then hear
what's stuck in my throat.

A howl
a groan, a rumble
of all the fast food you fed me
held down for too long.
Let me get this out and then
apologize for the rancid smell that clings
to our shoes.

My Heart

I hold my heart
in the morning
like it is all I have

close to the surface
unarmored
we are quiet

then I tuck it inside
it curls into the darkness
like an animal to sleep

sometimes it peeks out
but mostly I have to be content
knowing it is there
beating.

A Note to Whoever is in Charge

Sometimes I wish I had an extra orifice
to let the sadness out
a safety valve that wouldn't blow

but quietly release my gloom
without tear drops
without me falling to my knees.

A vent is all I ask for
discreet and easy to clean
maybe under an arm pit or between the toes

just a vent
to quietly release the weight of caring
to keep it all from piling up inside.

If Someone Told You

If someone told you the road you were driving on
was leading to the end of the world
would you stop the car?

If someone told you, that in fact, carbon dioxide
in your lungs made you want to breathe
would you want more of it?

If someone told you the rains will never stop
you would know they were wrong but might wonder
when *will* the water stop rising?

If someone told you the pavement was so hot
that it could fry an egg
you might wonder if any cook would find it helpful.

If someone told you that insect populations were collapsing
would you think it was good news
then wonder who will feed the birds?

If someone told you the earth was trying to tell you something
would you bow down to listen?

If someone told you that the road you were driving on
was leading to the end of the world
would you stop the car?

In Passing

How are you? you ask
and in the moment when fine could have worked
or OK would have done
there hung the weakening of the mid-day sun

I have, I say, a ticket for the momentum of a train
with its eye on the station
it passes the crossroads ringing
blows dust on backyard laundry
and ignores the brooks babbling below the trestles
its wheels are rolls of the snare
its diesel engines timpani boiling

Tremblor

The tremblor unsettles my teeth
my feet look for solid ground

the water will come soon
we will be battered by waves

how many times before we ask
why our homes are so brittle

it isn't with tears
but cracks that we fall apart

women sing praises to their mothers' mothers
while men charge into the darkness shouting.

Starry Night
An Ekphrastic Poem

It rolled in high on the sky
over our little town in the piedmont hills.
It came on a summer night

and I know it happened because we all saw it.
It woke us from our sleep and became our dream
bigger than we ever could have wondered

full of awe, full of fear
fuller than the sky
that held it in dimensions we had never seen before.

It rolled in
over and through us
and collectively we were transformed.

I had never heard the sound of light or tasted the moon.
I had never imagined that the touch of night's crystals could sing
or the wind could throw the stars.

But that is what happened as I
stood with my village in our central square
shoulder to shoulder, speechless, weeping

transformed by the spectacle of light
that radiated from a million stars
and reflected on our tear-streaked cheeks.

FOUR

Call to Kindness

What keeps us from letting
Kindness have her way?
I think she is waiting for us
for our sincere invitation
but we hold it back.
Do we think she isn't strong enough,
that she will not stay?

Imagine, if you can
a world that supports us
emotionally, unconditionally, totally
to the point where defenses fall down
and we walk into the day with the lightness of new shoes.

Imagine, if you will
offering a disarming smile
one that accepts, embraces, releases
the world from its fear
to the point that it smiles back
and we feel its light breeze in our hair.

Imagine, if you care
that you are the one to do this
for yourself
for others
for our world
so in need of your touch
your smile,
the one that lifts our hearts
the one that keeps us strong.

Tuber Tenacity

crazy bug-eyed potatoes
bet the farm
behind root cellar's door

white fingers
impossible to deny

Brownian Motion (pedesis)

Every sunny day
        indoors
                I see Brownian Motion.
The dusts,
they don't know what to do.

Some go right, down, over
                and then sideways
others go up, towards, under
        and then away.

They are more random than summer
water beetles,
        less concerned than cats
                on a comfy chair.

What does this tell us about Robert Brown
        whose name is associated
with this pedesis?

Was he undirected?

                Dodgy?

Unwilling to make

                decisions?

Poor man, his legacy is dust.

At least he is remembered
on a sunny day.

Lost Love

Linda Mastin, my first-grade girlfriend
which she will always be,
was kind, quiet and gentle
with sandy hair and a thin nose.
She had a pink raincoat
and short rubber boots.

Linda Mastin, we had so much in common
we both liked mud puddles
and were good at math,
you lived in a stucco house
and mine was stone,
I know there was much more
but it was so long ago.

Linda Mastin, it was a short affair
maybe a few weeks,
we left without words
people were watching,
I heard giggles and teasing
and our fresh glue fell apart.

Linda Mastin, a little cloud still lingers

were we made for each other
but just too soon?
Maybe in second grade
we would have been stronger,
we might have made it
but by that time I knew how to be a boy
and had run off with new loves.

The Birthday Party

Skipping through September like fairies
-delicate, careful, respectful-
dancing in the season of their sign
Virgos reign and all is in order,
or if it's not
there is a plan to make it so.

We see them in full glory this evening
with birthdays to celebrate;
(Celebrate, oh yes, they know how)
having arrived in lovely style
not because they thought anyone was looking
but because it satisfied them to be that way.

The house where the party is held,
the home of a Virgo,
holds the detailing of a fine watch
or calligraphy on parchment.
The spacing of the fork and knife,
the candles height and color, perfect.
No worries about a smudge on a wine glass,
all is cared for and Virgos can relax
yes, finally relax

while the others, Libra, Gemini and Taurus
breathe in the Virgo happiness
oblivious to what has happened
hoping this sweet moment might have something to
do with them
but they're not sure, so they smile
and check to see if they have crumbs on their shirts.

Closing for the Season

November sweeps the skies of blue
with feeble snow along northern shadows.

What was it thinking when it skipped
into October's meadows as if it were autumn's jewel?

Now it's hurry-up, close the shutters
cover the furniture, drain the pipes as the furnace cools.

Too soon December's bear will darken the doorway
wanting only to hear the faint sound of scurrying shoes

leaving through the back as the lights are turned off.

Thoughts About Winter

If winter was just sparkling snow under a blue sky
it would be always welcome.
If winter was just a good book by the fire
wouldn't that be sweet?

But cold frozen months barricaded by wool sweaters
and toe warmers and road slush hurled at you
from passing cars and a darkness that claims
so much of the clock's time are strong contenders
for our most debatable season.
We celebrate the solstice as the beginning
of the return but can forget long nights still stay
close, huddled about us like a lonely friend.
People who say they like winter often soften
on the edges as they age, the ice becomes more slippery
the fingers more numb, but they continue to talk
about the cleansing qualities of the cold,
its purity, its stillness.

And so it will stay this way
bright and clean
dark and dismal
quiet and reflective
relying on us to call it what we will
as the snow falls and the bears sleep
deep in their dens.

They Are Hiding Right in Front of Me

like the eye glasses giggling
above the visor of my cap

like the matching sock that snuck
to the back corner of my drawer

like sweet secrets to happiness
too simple to believe

they wait for me
for the moment

then we laugh at how easy
it is to be surprised

that they are so good at hiding
and I was so distracted
I could not see

Flurries

It is snowing

so lightly that each flake
could have its own name.

I try to introduce myself
but the wind wants nothing of it

and hurries the flurries
over the pasture hill.

Before I have them
I feel the loss

of their spritely friendship
that even without the wind

would have been fleeting.

Dogs and Writing

Her eyes are round and ears forward
the last six inches of her tail twitches
I know there is more to wag
but I show her my pen.
She says so what.
I say I am writing.
She says that's the problem.
I say you don't understand you're a dog.
She says you don't understand I'm a dog
and leaves still-tailed for another room.

One More Time

The sun came up again today
again the clouds hung thinly along the horizon
again night dark blue turned to pink
then orange, radiant orange.

Anticipation rose before the fire broke through
not with worry that it wouldn't come
but with marvel that it always comes
and for a moment,
not to take anything away from the sun's galactic durability,
I marvel too that I am here.

ABOUT THE AUTHOR

Phillip Mulligan grew up in the Genesee Valley of western New York State on a farm he was sure he would never leave; then he did. With his wife Susan, they moved a young family, some sheep and chickens to central Vermont where they lived for almost forty years. There Phillip made a career in building and renovating people's homes while fostering a writing practice along the way. They now live in Lebanon, NH.